PLAYER FACTFILE!

BEFORE YOU START, FILL IN YOUR FOOTY DETAILS!

MY NAME IS...

Fraser

MY FAVOURITE FOOTBALL TEAM IS...

Man Utd

MY FAVOURITE PLAYER IS...

De Gea

THE POSITION I PLAY IN IS...

GK

THE TEAMS I PLAY FOR ARE...

NOVA Star

MY FAVOURITE FOOTBALL BOOTS ARE...

Predators

THE BEST FOOTY CONSOLE GAME IS...

FiFa

MACMILLAN CHILDREN'S BOOKS

First published 2018 by Macmillan Children's Books
an imprint of Pan Macmillan
20 New Wharf Road, London N1 9RR
Associated companies throughout the world
www.panmacmillan.com

ISBN 978-1-5098-8008-9

Copyright © Kelsey Media 2018
Pictures copyright © Getty Images

1 3 5 7 9 8 6 4 2

A CIP catalogue record for this book is available from
the British Library.

Compiled by James Bandy
Designed by Darryl Tooth
Printed and bound by CPI Group (UK) Ltd, Croydon CR0 4YY

CONTENTS!

FIRST HALF

FIRST HALF!

It's time to kick-off your epic quiz book. Let's do this!

WORDSEARCH

Tick the box when you find each of these current or ex Prem teams!

✓	Arsenal	Aston Villa	
☐	Burnley	Chelsea	☐
☐	Everton	Fulham	☐
☐	Leeds	Leicester	☐
☐	Liverpool	Manchester City	

☐	Manchester United	Middlesbrough	
☐	Newcastle	Nottingham Forest	☐
☐	Southampton	Swansea	☐
☐	Tottenham	Watford	☐
☐	West Bromwich Albion	West Ham	✓

```
R V X U X W E S T H A M D T W A V D Z
D L B J B E K E E K N G Z Z S F N R V
K E U C N L E I C E S T E R J W E G V
J E R Y O I Q E W E E C Q B T X W Z J
J D N X T A Z C E D J D M G T J C B E
E S L Z T A X B S K O I P B A V A T X
M B E D I F D Y T B Y F X G R D S M W
A V Y X N U C J B Z G K K H S U T A H
N O X L G L H Z R P W Q J W E O L N P
C Y N X H H E D O C S H H Z N C E C K
H C M K A A L O M U X O K J A Z U H P
E T L D M M S V W S K Z L I L R L E S
S O I M F B E W I J G Q R L F A I S N
T T V D O D A V C K N K P O C Q X T S
E T E S R Z Z O H A T N G O X Q R E I
R E R F E N Q T A R S H Q V X Q Q R X
U N P N S C Y Y L R M T S C G M Q C K
N H O H T N G A B I I F O M Z H B I W
I A O J K F I Y I O D H U N E X Z T D
T M L P W M E F O J D U T B V I Q Y A
E X L R Y O W E N S L R H H Q I W V E
D K W M H S Q A Q X E G A S E P L C U
Y I J J N N E K U P S U M W V H S L E
N V Y D A S F B P B B Y P A E A A M A
M Q A U N W G N R U R J T T R H I M H
W R P A U N B K A O O Q O F T A Q U Y
D I W E Q L C K A D U O N O O E T W C
K S P G W H Q X D U G Q W R N E H K L
X P S H W D W P B T H I X D W W D J R
```

MATCH! 13

ZLATAN IBRAHIMOVIC

ALEXIS SANCHEZ

YAYA TOURE

CLUB SHARERS!

★ ★ ★ ★ ★ ★ ★ ★

Which club have these past World Cup stars all played for?

Barca

PEDRO

CESC FABREGAS

DANI ALVES

WORLD CUP...
NICKNAME GAME

Match these World Cup countries to their nickname!

ENGLAND — 1 — 1 AND C — A — SOCCEROOS

AUSTRALIA — 2 — 2 and A — B — SUPER EAGLES

BELGIUM — 3 — 3 and E — C — THREE LIONS

NIGERIA — 4 — 4 and B — D — BLUE SAMURAI

JAPAN — 5 — 5 and D — E — RED DEVILS

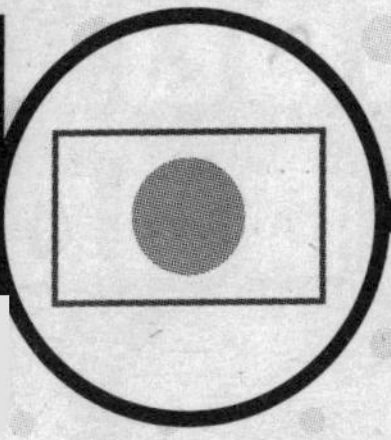

MATCH! 15

GOAL KINGS...

FILL IN THE SPACES!

Fill in the missing letters to work out these goal kings and the country they play for!

1. NAME M O R A T A
COUNTRY S P A I N

2. NAME K A N E
COUNTRY E N G L A N D

3. NAME M B A P P E
COUNTRY F R A N C E

4. NAME L U K A K U
COUNTRY B E L G I U M

5. NAME A G U E R O
COUNTRY A R G E N T I N A

6. NAME A U B A M E Y A N G
COUNTRY G A B O N

 16 MATCH!

WHO AM I?

↘ I was born in Salto, Uruguay, back in 1987.

↘ I started my career at Nacional before moving to Holland.

↘ In 2014 I joined Barcelona from Liverpool!

suarez

5 QUESTIONS ON...

LIONEL MESSI

FCB

0 · 1   18:34

1 In what year was Messi born
– 1986, 1987 or 1988?

1988

2 In what year did he
make his Barça debut
– 2000, 2002 or 2004?

2004

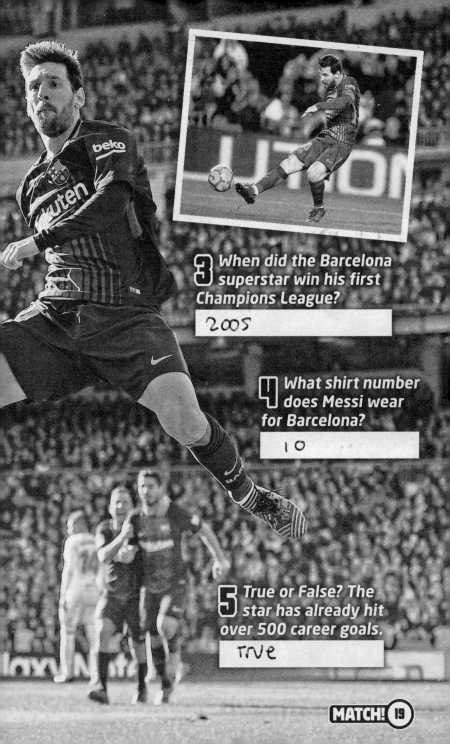

3 When did the Barcelona superstar win his first Champions League?

2005

4 What shirt number does Messi wear for Barcelona?

10

5 True or False? The star has already hit over 500 career goals.

True

1. Paulo Dybala

argentina

2. Marek Hamsik

slovakia

3. Radja Nainggolan

belgium

4. Miranda

Brazil

NAME THE COUNTRY!

Which countries do these Serie A stars come from?

5. Nani

Portugal

6. Pepe Reina

Spain

7. Kostas Manolas

Greece

8. Sami Khedira

germany

TRANSFER TRACKER!

Fill in the missing club of striker Gonzalo Higuain's career!

2005-07
River Plate

2007-13
Real Madrid

2013-16
Napoli

2016-
Juventus

Anthony Martial

James McCarthy

Joe Hart

FA CUP... ODD ONE OUT!

Which of these players has never won the FA Cup?

Mesut Ozil

Sergio Aguero

Kieran Gibbs

TRUE or FALSE?

Which of these statements are true, and which ones are totally made up?

1 The first ever FA Cup final was played way back in 1902.

2 No football club has won the FA Cup more than Arsenal.

3 Michael Owen holds the record for the fastest goal in an FA Cup final.

4 The FA Cup final was held at Old Trafford between 2002 and 2007.

5 Leicester have reached the final four times in their history but never won it.

5 QUESTIONS ON...

GARETH BALE

1 In what year was Bale born - 1987, 1989 or 1991?

2 With which club did the Wales ace start his career?

3 How many goals did he score in the 2014 Champions League final win over Atletico Madrid?

Presentación
BALE

4 Which manager signed him for Tottenham in 2007?

5 True or False? Bale broke the world transfer record when he signed for Real Madrid in 2013.

MAN. UNITED...

TRUE or FALSE?

Which of these statements are true, and which ones are totally made up?

1 When the club was formed, they were originally known as Newton Heath.

2 The Manchester giants didn't actually win the league between 1967 and 1993.

3 The Red Devils won the first five Premier League titles back in the 1990s.

4 Red Devils legend Sir Bobby Charlton is the club's all-time top scorer.

5 Paul Pogba moved from Juventus to United for a fee of £120 million back in 2016.

GUESS THE YEAR!

1. Premier League

2. FA Cup

3. Champions League

4. Community Shield

In which year do the pictures show United winning these trophies?

FLIP FOR IT

Tick the answer. You've got a 50/50 chance of getting it right!

1. Which club has won La Liga more times?

BARCELONA

REAL MADRID

2. Which of these Atletico Madrid stars has played for Chelsea?

FILIPE LUIS

JUANFRAN

3. Which club are nicknamed 'The Lions'?

ATHLETIC BILBAO

SEVILLA

4. Which other La Liga team plays in the city of Barcelona?

EIBAR

ESPANYOL

5. Which La Liga club plays at the Mestalla?

VILLARREAL

VALENCIA

6. Which player has played more La Liga games?

LIONEL MESSI

GARETH BALE

NAME THE CLUB

Which La Liga club's recent record is this?

2016-17	3rd
2015-16	3rd
2014-15	3rd
2013-14	1st
2012-13	3rd
2011-12	5th

Atletico Madrid.

1. Giants of France

GROUNDED!

Which Champions League regulars play at these amazing grounds? You're a quiz genius if you get them all right!

2. Madrid's second club

3. De Bruyne's home

4. Italy's Old Lady

LEGENDS...

WHO AM I?

Can you guess who this footy megastar is?

↘ I was a striker who started my career in Holland with Ajax.

↘ I moved to Inter Milan in Italy before joining The Gunners.

↘ I ripped it up with Ian Wright and then Thierry Henry.

Denis Berchamp

WHO STARTED WHERE?

Match the players with the clubs they started at!

WAYNE ROONEY

1

FRANK LAMPARD

2

ALAN SHEARER

3

DAVID BECKHAM

4

A	B	C	D
SOUTHAMPTON	MAN. UNITED	EVERTON	WEST HAM
3	4	1	2

NICKNAME GAME

Work out these Bundesliga teams' nicknames!

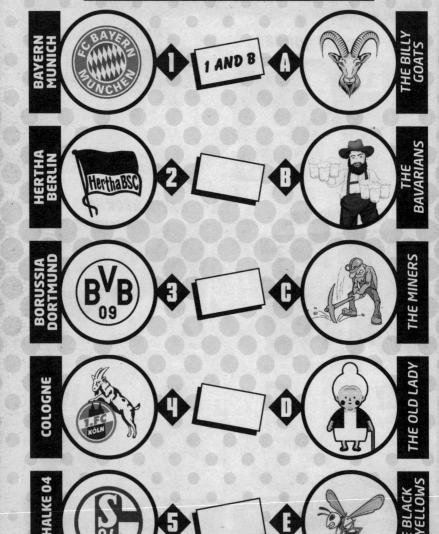

BAYERN MUNICH — 1 — 1 AND B — 4 — THE BILLY GOATS

HERTHA BERLIN — 2 — — B — THE BAVARIANS

BORUSSIA DORTMUND — 3 — — C — THE MINERS

COLOGNE — 4 — — D — THE OLD LADY

FC SCHALKE 04 — 5 — — E — THE BLACK AND YELLOWS

SOCCER SCRAMBLE

Rearrange these letters to find the Bundesliga club!

E I N T R A C H T
F R A N K F U R T

WORDSEARCH

Find the names of these Real Madrid legends in the grid!

Bale	Benzema
Butragueno	Carlos
Casillas	Di Stefano
Figo	Helguera
Hierro	Higuain

Marcelo	Modric
Pepe	Puskas
Ramos	Raul
Ronaldo	Salgado
Zamorano	Zidane

P E C J A T J N N G U U L Z T H V V X
C T Z S Z D U B A L E Y I Q I J N P Q
Y P V W B R B R V I E U M M Z R P G S
P U I X Z G K U F L T U P L M M C A H
D D L C S B O C T R H N W E R W K M M
P U J L P E W L O R V Q O K B S Z Z X
U Q U M E N I I N V A Y J B U E I I M
Q J S S J Z W H V G C G R P D I V D A
T R Y X M E T R O Y Q A U A C H N A R
K F M L A M H K U H V B M E U Z I N C

Z R C T W A   F N L M E E
I P Y J K P   K N O U N L
H L C X X G   J G L R I O
K L O J K E   C M F L Q S
R K U J Z E   R N H H V J
U U U K O Y   S C K Q R H
Y B P Z T Y   A A Q T A B
C M A Y Y A   L S Z Z M S
A O E Y R O   G I V O O K

R D L G P Q F I S W G O R A L H Q S I
L R H W F H E L G U E R A D L P C Q E
O I I F D I S T E F A N O O A I C Z D
S C D P J J G T S O T Q L Y S L H X H
V G E T E C D O H I E R R O A S H Z J
I D J Y A E A X J X S V E Z Q S I C O
Q Q Q H Y Z M O J O H I G U A I N P X
Z N H G K Z A M O R A N O C G T V E Y
L I I Z C B T L M R P Q Z U A Y Z P B
C P M C C E U B I R O N A L D O J E L

KEVIN DE BRUYNE

MO SALAH

DANIEL STURRIDGE

INTERNATIONAL...
CLUB SHARERS!

★ ★ ★ ★ ★ ★ ★ ★

Which Premier League club have these stars all played for?

ROMELU LUKAKU

NEMANJA MATIC

ANDRE SCHURRLE

INTERNATIONAL...

What Nationality?

Which country do these stars play for?
We've done one to get you started!

1
Thibaut Courtois

2
Anthony Martial

3
Wilfried Zaha

4
Sadio Mane

Ivory Coast

A

France

B

Senegal

C

Belgium

D

1 and D

MATCH! 39

1. Ben Woodburn

2. Christian Pulisic

3. Theo Hernandez

4. Kasper Dolberg

NAME THE COUNTRY!

Which national teams do these young superstars play for?

5. Jadon Sancho

6. Wilfred Ndidi

7. Gianluigi Donnarumma

8. Max Meyer

WONDERKIDS...

WHO AM I?

Can you guess the player?

↘ I was born in Wythenshawe, Manchester, in October 1997.

↘ I scored on my Europa League and Premier League debuts for United.

↘ I also scored on my England debut against Australia in 2016 and went to Euro 2016.

FIRST XI!

Can you answer 11 tough Man. City questions?

1. What stadium do City play their home games in?

2. Who is the manager of the Manchester club?

3. In which year did they first win the Premier League?

4. And who scored the late goal on the last day of the season to seal that title win?

5. The club are often known as City, but what is the other nickname they are known by?

6. What was City's awesome previous stadium called?

7. Who did they beat in the 2011 FA Cup Final?

8. Who was their manager for the 2011 FA Cup Final?

9. What country does wicked striker Gabriel Jesus play for?

10. Where did Man. City sign Raheem Sterling from – was it Arsenal or Liverpool?

11. What epic sports brand is Man. City's kit made by?

FILL IN THE SPACES!

Work out these Football League teams by filling in the gaps!

1. TEAM D _ R _ R Y
_ O U _ _ Y

2. TEAM P _ _ T S _ O _ _ H

3. TEAM L _ E _ S
U N _ T E _

4. TEAM P L _ M _ _ T H
A R _ Y _ E

5. TEAM A C _ R I _ G _ O N
S _ A L E _

NAME THE CLUB

Which club's recent record is this?

2016-17
Premier League — **18th**

2015-16
Championship — **4th**

2014-15
Premier League — **18th**

2013-14
Premier League — **16th**

2012-13
Championship — **2nd**

2011-12
Championship — **8th**

Robin van Persie

Lionel Messi

Shkodran Mustafi

WORLD CUP...

ODD ONE OUT!

Which of these stars has won the World Cup?

Antoine Griezmann

David Luiz

Alexis Sanchez

WORLD CUP...
FLIP FOR IT 👍

Tick the answer. You've got a 50/50 chance of getting it right!

1. How many times have England won the World Cup?

ONCE

NONE

2. Who will host the 2022 World Cup?

QATAR

UAE

3. When did Scotland last reach the World Cup finals?

1998

2002

4. Who won the 2010 World Cup in South Africa?

SPAIN

ARGENTINA

5. Which country has won more World Cups?

GERMANY

ARGENTINA

6. Where was the 2002 World Cup held?

CHINA

JAPAN & SOUTH KOREA

MATCH! 47

WORDFIT

Can you fit these 20 goal machines into this grid?

✔ Aguero	Aubameyang
Cavani	Costa
Dybala	Giroud
Griezmann	Higuain
Immobile	Jesus

Kane	Lacazette
Lewandowski	Lukaku
Messi	Morata
Neymar	Rashford
Ronaldo	Suarez

 48 MATCH!

PSG...

WHO AM I?

Can you guess the player?

↘ I started my career at Monaco and made my debut in 2015. ↘ After two seasons there, I moved clubs for £166 million! ↘ I'm a speedy striker who loves hitting the back of the net!

What Nationality?

Can you match these PSG stars to the countries they represent? We've done one for you!

1
Neymar

2
Angel Di Maria

3
Marco Verratti

4
Edinson Cavani

Italy

A

Uruguay

B

Argentina

C

Brazil

D

| 1 and D | | | |

MATCH! 51

NAME THE CLUB

Whose recent Prem record is this?

2016-17	6th
2015-16	5th
2014-15	4th
2013-14	7th
2012-13	1st
2011-12	2nd

NICKNAME GAME

Match these Prem clubs to their nickname!

SOUTHAMPTON  **1**  1 AND E **A**  **THE RED DEVILS**

MAN. UNITED **2**  **B** **THE TOFFEES**

LIVERPOOL  **3**  **C** REDS **THE REDS**

EVERTON  **4** **D** **THE CHERRIES**

BOURNEMOUTH  **5** **E**  **THE SAINTS**

MATCH! 53

FA CUP...
ACTION REPLAY ◀◀

See what you remember from the 2017 FA Cup Final by answering these tough questions!

1 Which Arsenal player scored the first goal of the game?

2 Who played in goal for The Gunners?

3 What was the score at half-time?

4 Which Chelsea star was sent off in the second half?

5 What was the final score?

SOCCER SCRAMBLE

Rearrange the letters to find the name of a big world star!

WHO STARTED WHERE?

Match these awesome players with the club they started at!

NEYMAR

1

ROMELU LUKAKU

2

ALVARO MORATA

3

TONI KROOS

4

A

REAL MADRID

B

ANDERLECHT

C

BAYERN MUNICH

D

SANTOS

TRUE or FALSE?

Try to work out which of these statements are true, and which are totally made up!

1 Legendary gaffer Jose Mourinho had two spells in charge of Chelsea.

2 The Blues' title win in 2017 was their 6th Premier League title win in total.

3 Alvaro Morata became Chelsea's record signing when he joined the club in 2017.

4 Legendary midfielder Frank Lampard is the club's all-time top goalscorer.

5 N'Golo Kante cost the club £45 million when he signed from Leicester in 2016.

CHELSEA...

What Nationality?

Match these Chelsea stars to the countries they represent! We've done the first one for you!

1 Antonio Rudiger

2 Tiemoue Bakayoko

3 Michy Batshuayi

4 Victor Moses

France
A

Nigeria
B

Germany
C

Belgium
D

1 and C

MATCH! 59

WORDSEARCH

Try to find the names of these 20 La Liga stars in the grid!

Aduriz	Aspas
Bruno	Carrasco
Griezmann	Illarramendi
Koke	Kroos
Lato	Messi

Navas	Oblak
Parejo	Ramos
Rakitic	Ronaldo
Soriano	Suarez
Williams	Zaza

```
H V R T Q H E W Z I S S E M A B N Z A
R P Q Y C N D E I B R U N O D Z Q P I
S P Y N P B Q O B W U D N L U Y G D A
A I H Q Y I M F T J P N V V R X P T O
V K T X E P S E K B A D C Z I I G S K
A P N V Z S B K O M Y V N Q Z O Z A N
N U T C R N C A Z N W B A B L L Y P A
I C C A P D W E G A U V F G K H E S I
Y T S R O D I U J U T Y J V O H Z A D
D L E R Q R Z D E V U F F S K R J Z N
B J Z A G F                 V E S M M E
B W R S F F                 T Z R Z R M
Y I A C L W                 U Z X I A A
G U M O C D                 L S J V K R
S Q O D J F                 E C A A I R
B D S K Y S                 Z F L H T A
F Q E P U G                 H B M T I L
E A P Z O E                 O B G S C L
Q Q Y J Y G                 C H C U L I
V O A N G C D R I T U N X P F G A N C
L D X I V P J J Z N U T G F Y P R T E
Z L G Y T L T G Q N U M Q V P Z E A V
T A H U I U B K R O O S V R V A Z F O
P N R K W I L L I A M S P I K Z K W J
H O E B J L I B O P Y A O E R A L J E
X R H V L T K Q A I A R Z G B S S B R
B W U A A D N Y Q X X L K Z D I E K A
X K T V Q M S P D O N A I R O S K H P
N O Z R K Z N W C M Y G J J Y K G E U P
```

LaLiga

SAMUEL UMTITI

MATHIEU VALBUENA

HUGO LLORIS

CHAMPIONS LEAGUE...

CLUB SHARERS!

★ ★ ★ ★ ★ ★ ★

Which Champions League regular did these stars all play for?

DEJAN LOVREN

MIRALEM PJANIC

KARIM BENZEMA

TRUE or FALSE?

Which of these statements are true, and which ones are totally made up?

1 North London giants Arsenal have never won the Champions League.

2 Barcelona have won more Champions League titles than massive rivals Real Madrid.

3 Leicester City reached the quarter-finals of the Champions League in 2016-17.

4 The Champions League used to be known as the UEFA Cup before 1992.

5 The 2017 Champions League final was played at Cardiff's Millennium Stadium.

FILL IN THE SPACES!

Work out these football legends by filling in the gaps in their names!

1. NAME D A _ I _ I _ / _ E C _ _ A M

2. NAME R _ N A _ _ O

3. NAME _ I D _ _ R / D _ O _ B A

4. NAME T _ _ _ R R Y / H _ N _ Y

5. NAME F R _ N C E _ C _ / T _ _ T _

LEGENDS...
TRANSFER TRACKER!

Can you fill in the gap of Frank Lampard's awesome career?

1995-2001
West Ham

1995-96
Swansea (Loan)

2001-2014
?

2014-2015
Man. City

2015-16
New York City

5 QUESTIONS ON...
JUVENTUS

1 The club have quite a strange nickname, but what is it?

2 The club got their famous black and white stripes from which English club?

JUVENTUS

3 In which Italian city do Juve play their home games?

4 In what year was the club formed – 1887, 1897 or 1907?

5 In 2016, who did they sell for a then world record transfer fee?

NICKNAME GAME

What are these Serie A clubs' nicknames?

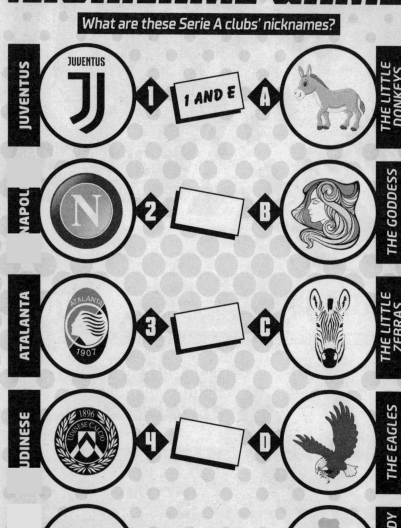

JUVENTUS — 1 — 1 AND E — A — THE LITTLE DONKEYS

NAPOLI — 2 — B — THE GODDESS

ATALANTA — 3 — C — THE LITTLE ZEBRAS

UDINESE — 4 — D — THE EAGLES

LAZIO — 5 — E — THE OLD LADY

NAME THE CLUB

Which club's recent Serie A record is this?

Season	Position
2016-17	2nd
2015-16	3rd
2014-15	2nd
2013-14	2nd
2012-13	6th
2011-12	7th

TRUE or FALSE?

Which of these statements are true, and which ones are totally made up?

1 England have never won the European Championships, or even reached the final.

2 Flying Manchester City winger Leroy Sane plays his internatioanl footy with Germany.

3 The 2022 World Cup finals will be held in Qatar and will start in November.

4 Brazil won the 2014 World Cup, beating Argentina 1-0 in the final.

5 Manchester United's Marcus Rashford is the youngest player ever to represent England.

SOCCER SCRAMBLE

Rearrange the letters to spell this international team!

WORDFIT

See if you can fit these young stars into the grid!

Abraham	Alexander-Arnold
Davies	De Ligt
Dembele	Diaz
Dolberg	Donnarumma
Edwards	Foden

Fosu-Mensah	Gomez
Locatelli	Malcom
Mbappe	Ndidi
Nelson	Pulisic
Rashford	Tielemans

MBAPPE

ARSENAL...

WHO AM I?

Read the clues to work out who this Arsenal star is!

↘ I was born back in France in 1991.

↘ I joined Arsenal from Lyon.

↘ I am a striker and France international.

FLIP FOR IT

Tick the answer. You've got a 50/50 chance of getting it right!

1. Who holds the record for most Arsenal goals?

IAN WRIGHT

THIERRY HENRY

2. What's the name of Arsenal's awesome old stadium?

HIGHBURY

HIGH VALE

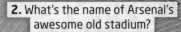

3. How much did they pay to sign Danny Welbeck?

£12 MILLION

£16 MILLION

4. What nationality is midfielder Granit Xhaka?

SWISS

POLISH

5. How many times have The Gunners won the FA Cup?

12

13

6. From which club did they sign defender Sead Kolasinac?

SCHALKE

HAMBURG

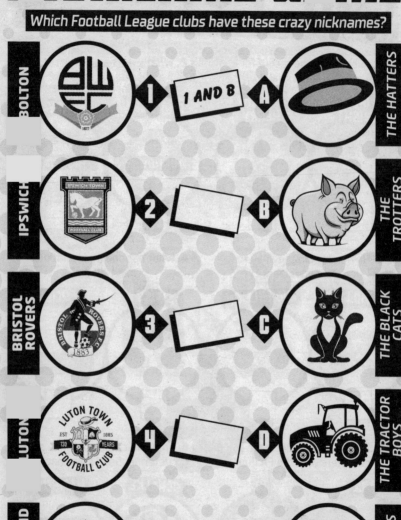

FOOTBALL LEAGUE...
NICKNAME GAME

Which Football League clubs have these crazy nicknames?

BOLTON — 1 — **1 AND 8** — A — **THE HATTERS**

IPSWICH — 2 — B — **THE TROTTERS**

BRISTOL ROVERS — 3 — C — **THE BLACK CATS**

LUTON — 4 — D — **THE TRACTOR BOYS**

SUNDERLAND — 5 — E — **THE PIRATES**

76 **MATCH!**

Rob Green

Britt Assombalonga

Matej Vydra

Which of these stars has not played in the Premier League?

George Boyd

Ali Al Habsi

Mile Jedinak

SIMON MIGNOLET

DANNY WELBECK

JERMAIN DEFOE

FOOTBALL LEAGUE...

CLUB SHARERS!

★ ★ ★ ★ ★ ★ ★

Which Football League club have these stars all played for?

JORDAN HENDERSON

JAMES McCLEAN

JORDAN PICKFORD

HALF-TIME BREAK!

Quizzed out?

Take a rest and have

a go at these

cool activities!

DESIGN YOUR OWN

MEGA KITS!

We love cool kits!
Why not create
your own here?

BUILD YOUR...
DREAM TEAM!

Ever fancied being the boss?
Well here's your chance!
Pick your fantasy team
from these stars,
or choose your own!

GOALKEEPERS
CHOOSE ONE

Thibaut Courtois

David De Gea

Ederson

Hugo Lloris

Kasper Schmeichel

Other... fill below

GK

FB

FB

CENTRE-BACKS
CHOOSE TWO

Toby Alderweireld

Cesar Azpilicueta

Eric Bailly

Laurent Koscielny

Harry Maguire

Nicolas Otamendi

Antonio Rudiger

Mamadou Sakho

John Stones

Virgil Van Dijk

Jan Vertonghen

Other... fill below

FULL-BACKS
CHOOSE TWO

Marcos Alonso

Leighton Baines

Hector Bellerin

Nathaniel Clyne

Sead Kolasinac

Benjamin Mendy

Andrew Robertson

Danny Rose

Antonio Valencia

Kyle Walker

Other... fill above

CB

CB

BUILD YOUR...
DREAM TEAM!

MIDFIELDERS

CHOOSE TWO

Eric Dier

Cesc Fabregas

Fernandinho

Ilkay Gundogan

N'Golo Kante

Nemanja Matic

Wilfred Ndidi

Paul Pogba

Victor Wanyama

Granit Xhaka

Other... fill top right

STRIKERS
CHOOSE ONE
Roberto Firmino

Gabriel Jesus

Harry Kane

Romelu Lukaku

Alvaro Morata

Other… fill below

S

ATTACKING MIDFIELDERS
CHOOSE THREE
Dele Alli

Kevin De Bruyne

Christian Eriksen

Eden Hazard

Riyad Mahrez

Sadio Mane

Anthony Martial

Henrikh Mkhitaryan

Mesut Ozil

Mohamed Salah

Alexis Sanchez

Leroy Sane

David Silva

Raheem Sterling

Willian

Other… fill bottom left

BUILD YOUR... DREAM TEAM!

Now fill in your starting line-up and colour in your Dream Team shirts, too! What an amazing team!

SECOND HALF!

After that break, you'll be ready for the second half of puzzles & quizzes!

ACTION REPLAY

How much do you remember about this epic 2014 World Cup clash between Brazil and Germany?

1 What was the final score in this game?

2 What colour kit did Germany wear that day?

3 Was this in the quarter-finals or semi-finals of World Cup 2014?

4 True or False? Germany were 5-0 up after 29 minutes.

5 How many different players scored for Germany – five, six or seven?

TRUE or FALSE?

Which of these statements are true, and which ones are totally made up?

1 Tottenham and England superstar Harry Kane once played on loan at Millwall.

2 Awesome Argentina goal machine Sergio Aguero joined Man. City from Atletico Madrid.

3 Brazil wizard Neymar joined PSG for a fee of £300 million from Barcelona.

4 Real Madrid and Portugal legend Cristiano Ronaldo has scored over 600 career goals.

5 Lethal Pierre-Emerick Aubameyang plays his international football with Mali.

WHO STARTED WHERE?

Which clubs did these heroes start their career with?

MICHY BATSHUAYI

1

ANTOINE GRIEZMANN

2

ANTHONY MARTIAL

3

CHRISTIAN BENTEKE

4

A

OLYMPIQUE LYONNAIS

LYON

B

STANDARD LIEGE

C

REAL SOCIEDAD

D

Genk
we're magic

GENK

ÄNAGRAMS!

Rearrange the letters to find the Bayern legends!

1. LAMENU REENU

2. TARROU DILVA

3. SATM MUELSHM

4. HAMTOS LEMLUR

5. AIDDV BLAAA

WHO AM I?

Can you work out who this Bayern legend is?

↘ I was born in Poland in August 1988. ↘ joined Bayern from Borussia Dortmund. ↘ I'm a powerful and deadly goalscorer.

IN THE BOX!

How much do you know about the world's toughest league?

1

It seems like it's been going forever, but in which year did the Premier League begin?

A	1991
B	1992
C	1993

4

Which one of these clubs has been relegated from the Premier League?

A	Arsenal
B	Everton
C	Man. City

Which mega club has won the Premier League the most times?

A	Man. United
B	Chelsea
C	Man. City

Which of these teams has never won the Premier League?

A	Leicester
B	Liverpool
C	Blackburn

How many matches does each team play in a Premier League season?

A	38
B	40
C	42

SOCCER SCRAMBLE

Rearrange the letters to find the recent FA Cup winners!

W I G A N

A H _ _ I C

Alexis Sanchez

Diego Costa

Curtis Davies

FA CUP... ODD ONE OUT!

Which of these players hasn't scored in an FA Cup final?

Jason Puncheon

Jamie Vardy

Theo Walcott

LEONARDO BONUCCI

ALVARO MORATA

ARTURO VIDAL

CLUB SHARERS!

★ ★ ★ ★ ★ ★ ★ ★

Which top team have these footy superstars all played for?

JUVENTUS

DANI ALVES

FERNANDO LLORENTE

KINGSLEY COMAN

WHO AM I?

Use the clues to work out the massive footy superstar!

↘ I used to play for Inter Milan.

↘ I joined Barcelona from The Reds.

↘ I'm a Brazil-iant goalscorer!

LIVERPOOL...
WORDSEARCH

Can you find these 20 Liverpool legends hidden in the grid?

Aldridge		Alonso
Barnes		Beardsley
Carragher		Coutinho
Dalglish		Dudek
Fowler		Gerrard

Hamann		Henderson
Hyypia		Mascherano
Owen		Reina
Rush		Salah
Suarez		Torres

```
G O F W G K L G W J P D T J I F O V H
F O W L E R X F R J H X D F C I Y S H
R V M M X S R E I N A W B Q D C A E
K S F J N A H A M A N N L H D V N L E
M A U O X K U H V M L J U Y S C B D R
B Y V K H A S C D A L G L I S H Z R U
L I I P K Y O Y G T L M Y T V W J I S
D V Y M N B E A R D S L E Y T H A D H
U W W B W L G A N M R Y R Z M O C G L
D K N G Y N R K P P O Q H U L A V E V
E Y P P G E                 Y U C S R R
K D C L D R                 S Y W O C N
P X S R H A                 V J P V O D
E A X L Y Z                 B R P I Q P
C W K A X C                 A Q B Z A K
N W Q J R O                 V C N N U P
G N W K U U                 C P J H B I
O E R D E T                 N T P G C W
D C F X B I                 S D Z H V R
N C Z M W N N V P W I D P F V U D V E
F F N X Q H Y M O M C J D G N Z S P Z
A L O N S O J Z D W M X I E E V B Y G
F S G T O R R E S B E R Q R N T A Z U
C S V E G D G K T Q O N A R I R R M W
G K U R Z F B P Z V I U L A B A N O E
W C A R R A G H E R S J D R Z T E B Y
C Z V H E N D E R S O N Q N D R W S Y
W Q H D U J T M T K E K K S U P R P W
H S A L A H W C W M A S C H E R A N O
```

YOU'LL NEVER WALK ALONE

LIVERPOOL
FOOTBALL CLUB

EST · 1892 ®

FILL IN THE SPACES!

Fill in the gaps to work out the names of these Bundesliga teams!

1. TEAM
⬜ O R ⬜ S ⬜ I ⬜
⬜ O R ⬜ M ⬜ N ⬜

2. TEAM
H O ⬜ F E ⬜ H ⬜ ⬜ M

3. TEAM
B A ⬜ E ⬜ N
⬜ U ⬜ C ⬜

4. TEAM
W ⬜ L ⬜ S ⬜ U R ⬜

5. TEAM
⬜ A Y ⬜ R
⬜ E ⬜ ⬜ R K ⬜ S E ⬜

BUNDESLIGA...

TRANSFER TRACKER!

Can you fill in the gap of class midfielder Arturo Vidal's career?

2005-07
Colo-Colo

2007-11
B. Leverkusen

2011-15
Juventus

2015-
?

1. Zinedine Zidane

france

2. Raul

spain

3. Gabriel Batistuta

argentina

4. Luis Figo

portogui

NAME THE COUNTRY!

Which countries did these footy legends play for?

5. Diego Forlan

vrugui

6. Ronaldo

brazil

7. Carlos Valderrama

corumbia

8. Diego Maradona

argentina

LEGENDS...

WHO AM I?

Try to guess this legendary player from the clues and pic!

↘ I started my career at Southampton. ↘ I won the Premier League at Blackburn. ↘ I ended my career at my hometown club.

5 QUESTIONS ON...
CHAMPIONS

1 **Which English team won the Champions League in 2012?**

UEF

2 **Which club has won the competition the most times?**

real madria

3 **Who did Barcelona beat to win the 2014-15 Champions League?**

joventus

LEAGUE

4 Who has won the CL more times
- AC Milan or Man. United?

5 True or False? Nottingham Forest
have won the European Cup twice.

True

Saul

Jan Oblak

Gabi

ATLETICO MADRID...
ODD ONE OUT!

Who is the only Atletico star who has played in the Prem?

Juanfran

Stefan Savic

Angel Correa

WHO AM I?

Use the clues to guess who this Atletico legend is!

↘ I joined Atletico Madrid in 2010.

↘ I play international football for Uruguay.

↘ I'm a defender who loves a battle.

NICKNAME GAME

Which awesome La Liga teams have these nicknames?

ATLETICO MADRID — 1 — **1 AND D** — A — THE MERINGUES

CELTA VIGO — 2 — B — THE YELLOW SUBMARINE

REAL MADRID — 3 — C — THE HEY

VILLARREAL — 4 — D — THE MATTRESS MAKERS

VALENCIA — 5 — E — THE LITTLE CELTS

LA LIGA...

What Nationality?

Match these La Liga stars to the countries they represent. We've done one to start you off!

1

Diego Godin

2

Inaki Williams

3

Samuel Umtiti

4

Luka Modric

Croatia

A

Uruguay

B

Spain

C

France

D

1 and B

MATCH! 111

WORDFIT

Try to fit all these wicked countries in the grid!

✓ Algeria	Australia
✓ Belgium	Brazil
✓ Chile	Croatia
Denmark	England
France	Germany

Ghana	Holland
Iceland	Japan
Nigeria	Northern Ireland
Portugal	Scotland
Spain	Wales

 112 MATCH!

CHILE

belgium

algeria

japan

What Nationality?

Which countries do these wonderkids come from?
We've done the first one to start you off!

1

Arthur

2

Marcus Edwards

3

Brahim Diaz

4

Jeff Reine-Adelaide

Spain

A

England

B

France

C

Brazil

D

1 and D

SOCCER SCRAMBLE

Rearrange the letters to reveal this young Prem star!

P			L	F		D		N

ÄNAGRAMS!

Rearrange the letters to revel these recent Spurs stars!

1. RAYHR NAKE

2. CIVROT MANAWAY

3. UHOG RILLSO

4. BOTY WEELIDRADLER

5. NANDY SORE

WHO AM I?

Read the clues and try to work out who the Spurs ace is!

⬂ I was born April 11, 1996 in Milton Keynes.

⬂ I joined Spurs for £5 million in 2015.

⬂ I wear the No.20 shirt for the club.

IN THE BOX!

How much do you know about Italy's league?

1
Which awesome club has won the most Serie A league titles?

A	Roma	
B	AC Milan	
C	Juventus	

4
Which wicked stadium has the largest capacity in Serie A?

A	**Allianz** (Juventus)	
B	**San Siro** (Inter & AC Milan)	
C	**Stadio Olimpico** (Lazio & Roma)	

2 Keeper Gianluigi Donnarumma started his career at which club?

A	AC Milan
B	Roma
C	Inter Milan

3 Serie A giants Juventus come from which Italian city?

A	Venice
B	Florence
C	Turin

5 Inter Milan star Mauro Icardi plays for which country?

A	Italy
B	Chile
C	Argentina

WORLD CUP...

FILL IN THE SPACES!

Fill in the gaps to reveal these World Cup stars!

1. NAME [ ] D E [ ] H [ ] Z [ ] [ ] D

2. NAME [ ] T O [ ] I [ ] R O [ ] S

3. NAME N [ ] [ ] M [ ] R

4. NAME G E R [ ] R [ ] [ ] I Q E

5. NAME H U [ ] O L L O [ ] I [ ]

120 MATCH!

WORLD CUP...
TRANSFER
TRACKER!

Fill in the missing club of World Cup winner Mesut Ozil!

2006-2008
Schalke

2008-2010
Werder Bremen

2010-2013
Real Madrid

2013-
?

Jamie Vardy

Diego Costa

Zlatan Ibrahimovic

GOAL KINGS...
ODD ONE OUT!

Who is the only goal machine who hasn't won the Premier League?

Cristiano Ronaldo

Edin Dzeko

Wayne Rooney

TRUE or FALSE?

Try to work out which of these statements are true, and which are totally made up!

1 Man. City hero Sergio Aguero has never won the Premier League Golden Boot.

2 England strikers Harry Kane and Jamie Vardy played together at Leicester.

3 PSG and goal machine Neymar started his career at Barcelona.

4 Barcelona wizard Lionel Messi once scored 60 goals in one season.

5 Roberto Firmino signed for Liverpool from Borussia Dortmund.

ACTION REPLAY

How much do you remember about this massive game between England and Iceland at Euro 2016?

?

1 Who was fouled to win England's penalty in the fourth minute?

2 And which player scored the resulting spot-kick?

3 What was the score at half-time?

4 True or False? Gylfi Sigurdsson scored for Iceland.

5 Who played in goal for England?

TRUE or FALSE?

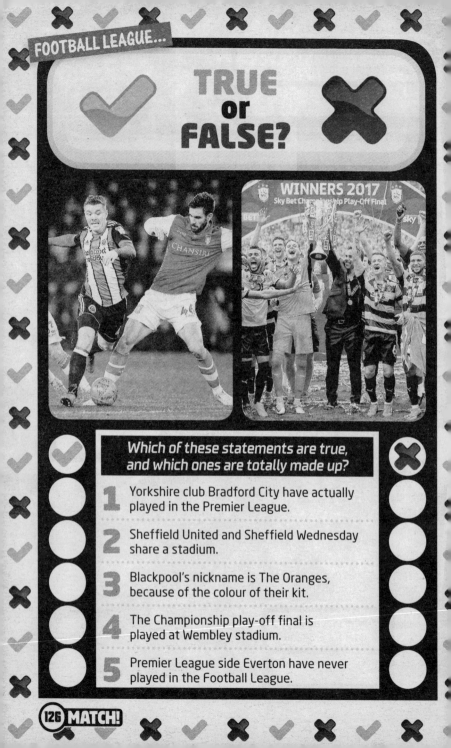

WINNERS 2017
Sky Bet Championship Play-Off Final

Which of these statements are true, and which ones are totally made up?

1 Yorkshire club Bradford City have actually played in the Premier League.

2 Sheffield United and Sheffield Wednesday share a stadium.

3 Blackpool's nickname is The Oranges, because of the colour of their kit.

4 The Championship play-off final is played at Wembley stadium.

5 Premier League side Everton have never played in the Football League.

GUESS THE YEAR!

1. Newcastle

2. Burnley

3. Bournemouth

4. Leicester

Can you guess when these teams won the Championship?

FILL IN THE SPACES!

Fill in the gaps to work out these FA Cup-winning clubs!

1. 2017 A _ S _ N _ L

2. 2016 M _ _ C _ E _ S _ R U _ I _ E _

3. 2013 W _ G _ _ _ T _ L _ T _ C

4. 2012 C H _ L _ _ A

5. 2011 _ A _ C _ E S T _ R C _ _ Y

WHO AM I?

Work out this FA Cup winner from the clues!

↘ I've won the FA Cup a massive five times. ↘ I've won it with Chelsea and Arsenal. ↘ I'm a keeper from the Czech Republic.

WORDSEARCH

Can you find these 20 footy megastars in the grid?

Bale	Cavani
Coutinho	De Bruyne
Dybala	Griezmann
Hazard	Isco
Kane	Kante

Kroos	Lewandowski
Mbappe	Messi
Modric	Neymar
Pogba	Ramos
Ronaldo	Salah

```
Q P D S I K Z P Q I E F H G L Y J B P
X W M H I U U Z B Q O O C P I X V H A L
W Y P G T E M Q R G G X J I K D V O T
H V Q O D H S V A Z V S C A V A N I A
N S V N Z S R X Z G R I E Z M A N N H
W J R T V X E L M R Z H F G S T I P D
K V C R E L J P O G B A V H S M M F R
X A S Z A Y N D K A N T E D U Q C W K
Q G N B Q R N M L E W A N D O W S K I
Y E A E X R P R D H U R Z M Z M Y N R
C F R O N A L D O F S A L A H V R M E
Z B L V C G             I K O P Q M
Z X L O R F             I W Y B U B
B A Q E K L             D Q O R Q A
R P O Z D G             C D K B B P
Z J R F G G             S M D J A P
B K P A O M             X K C Z T E
R Z V M S Z             T R O R Y C
M V F A L S U K S Q L D E B R U Y N E
O O T E M X Q P R N Z K L R A M O S I
D E E Q W Q G M Z O V E J W Z D H G N
R S Z U L C P X U W O N T O H Y W M Q
I S C O I R O L J J V S S A A B P R C
C R Z F D J D U W A D W B M Z A X A K
O N E Y M A R X T C N D E E A L A W W
F H B M E S S I Q I U L H B R A V C U
U Z B R V L R O W J N M I U D Z Y Y C
H T T M V U H G K W Q H S F K Q Q G W
C C M F U M Y F R J A C O I H C Q A B
```

Neymar

Philippe Coutinho

Fernandinho

BRAZIL...

ODD ONE OUT!

Who is the only Brazil star who has won the Premier League?

Roberto Firmino

Paulinho

Marcelo

BRAZIL...

TRUE or FALSE?

Which of these statements are true, and which ones are totally made up?

1 Total football legend Pele used to play international footy for Brazil.

2 Brazil have won the wicked World Cup trophy a total of three times.

3 The World Cup finals have never been hosted in Brazil.

4 Brazil have qualified for every World Cup finals since it started in 1930.

5 PSG goal machine Neymar has already scored more than 50 goals for Brazil.

PREMIER LEAGUE...

WHO AM I?

Can you guess this footy megastar?

↘ I'm an England international.

↘ My first club was Sheffield United.

↘ I joined Man. City from Spurs.

walker

MATCH!

WHO STARTED WHERE?

Match the players with the clubs they started at!

THEO WALCOTT

1

DELE ALLI

2

DANNY DRINKWATER

3

KASPER SCHMEICHEL

4

A

SOUTHAMPTON

B
MANCHESTER CITY
MAN. CITY

C
MK DONS
MK DONS

D
MANCHESTER UNITED
MAN. UNITED

FIRST XI!

What do you know about the Champions League?

1. How many teams take part in the group stage of the competition?

2. Which English club has won the CL the most times?

3. Which CL regular does Sergio Busquets play for?

4. Which English club won the Champions League in 2005?

5. In 2008, which two English clubs faced each other in the Champions League final?

6. And which team lifted the trophy on that night?

7. With how many clubs has Cristiano Ronaldo won the CL?

8. True or False? Chelsea have never won the CL.

9. When was the last time Wembley hosted the final – 2013, 2015 or 2017?

10. Which team won the 2017 Champions League final?

11. And which huge world star scored twice that night?

What Nationality?

Which countries do these stars play for? We've done one to start you off!

1
Alvaro Morata

2

Luis Suarez

3

Andre Silva

4

Paulo Dybala

A
Argentina

B
Spain

C
Portugal

D
Uruguay

I and B

TRANSFER TRACKER!

Fill in the missing club that ace striker Romelu Lukaku has played for!

2009-2011
Anderlecht

2011-2014
Chelsea

2012-13
W. Brom (loan)

2013-17
?

2017-
Man. United

ÄNAGRAMS!

Rearrange the letters to work out these Spain internationals!

1. VIADD DEEGA

2. VALOAR TAMARO

3. GISREO OARMS

4. DOGIE COATS

5. ODRIJ BALA

FLIP FOR IT

Tick the answer. You've got a 50/50 chance of getting it right!

1. Which Spain star has won more international caps?

SERGIO RAMOS

SERGIO BUSQUETS

2. Who scored the only goal in the 2010 World Cup Final?

ANDRES INIESTA

FERNANDO TORRES

3. What was the score in the Euro 2012 final against Italy?

4-0

3-1

4. Who is Spain's manager?

IKER CASILLAS

JULEN LOPETEGUI

5. Which player has scored more international goals?

DAVID SILVA

ANDRES INIESTA

6. Which club does Spain ace Saul play for?

ATHLETIC BILBAO

ATLETICO MADRID

BUNDESLIGA...
WORDFIT

Find these stars who've played in the Bundesliga!

Alaba	Aubameyang
Burki	Fahrmann
Forsberg	Hummels
Kagawa	Keita
Leno	Lewandowski ✓

Martinez	Muller
Reus	Ribery
Robben	Rodriguez
Sokratis	Sommer
Vidal	Werner

LEWANDOWSKI

1. Shinji Okazaki

2. Luis Suarez

3. Nani

4. Sergio Busquets

NAME THE COUNTRY!

Which countries do these World Cup heroes play for?

5. Fernandinho

6. Ivan Rakitic

7. Javier Hernandez

8. Radja Nainggolan

WORLD CUP...
SOCCER SCRAMBLE

Rearrange the letters to find the World Cup-winning star!

| M | | R | | O | | G | | T | | | |

MATCH! 145

Lionel Messi

Ever Banega

Angel Di Maria

ARGENTINA...

ODD ONE OUT!

Which Argentina star is the only one who has played in the Prem?

Paulo Dybala

Enzo Perez

Gonzalo Higuain

TRUE or FALSE?

Which of these statements are true, and which ones are totally made up?

1 Argentina won the World Cup in 2014, beating Germany 1-0 in the final.

2 Barcelona legend Lionel Messi is Argentina's all-time top goalscorer.

3 Argentina have won the World Cup more times than any other country.

4 Footy legend Diego Maradona used to play international football for Argentina.

5 Awesome striker Sergio Aguero is also Argentina's captain.

1. This stadium isn't Messi

2. It's called the Mestalla

3. The Yellow Submarines?

4. This is Real-ly good

CHAMPIONS LEAGUE...
FLIP FOR IT

Tick the answer. You've got a 50/50 chance of getting it right!

1. Which club has won the Champions League more times?

AC MILAN

□

BARCELONA

□

2. Who was the Champions League's top scorer in 2016-17?

LIONEL MESSI

□

CRISTIANO RONALDO

□

3. Where will the 2018-19 Champions League final be played?

WANDA METROPOLITANO

□

BERNABEU

□

4. Have Arsenal ever won the Champions League?

YES

□

NO

□

5. Which country do Champions League regulars FC Basel come from?

AUSTRIA

□

SWITZERLAND

□

6. Who is the only team ever to win the CL two years in a row?

BARCELONA

□

REAL MADRID

□

(150) **MATCH!**

WHO AM I?

Read the clues to guess this Champions League winner!

↘ I've won the CL more than once.

↘ I'm an ace defender who scores goals too!

↘ I play international footy for Spain.

1. Ryan Giggs

2. Deco

3. Michel Salgado

4. Francesco Totti

NAME THE COUNTRY!

Which countries did these football heroes play for?

5. Dennis Bergkamp

6. Michael Ballack

7. Romario

8. Roy Keane

SOCCER SCRAMBLE

Rearrange the letters to find an England football legend!

G _ _ Y

L I _ _ K R

LEGENDS...

What Nationality?

**Which country did these footy legends play for?
We've answered one to get you going!**

1

Fernando Hierro

2

Hugo Sanchez

3

Marcelo Salas

4

Fernando Redondo

Mexico

A

Spain

B

Argentina

C

Chile

D

1 and B

FULL TIME!

It's the end of the quiz! Take a break and do some cool activities!

DESIGN YOUR OWN

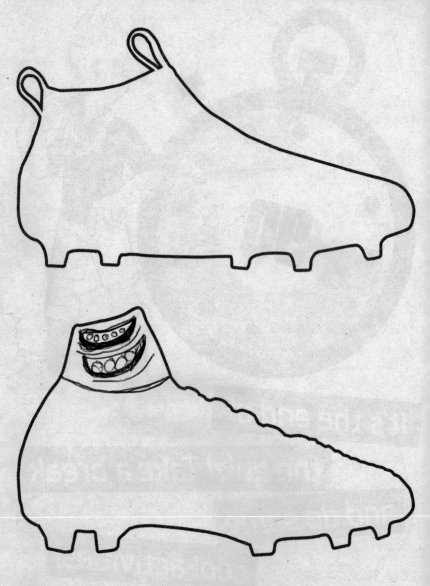

ACE BOOTS!

Love cool boots? Grab some pencils and design your own!

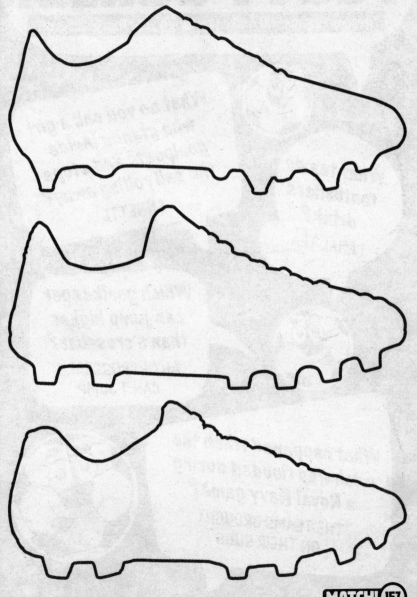

FOOTY JOKES!

These epic gags will make you laugh your footy socks off!

What do you call a girl who stands inside goalposts and stops the ball rolling away?

ANNETTE

What tea do footballers drink?

PENAL-TEA.

Which goalkeeper can jump higher than a crossbar?

ANY – CROSSBARS CAN'T JUMP

What happened when the pitch was flooded during a Royal Navy game?

THE TEAMS BROUGHT ON THEIR SUBS

England manager Gareth Southgate has set up a friendly match with Iceland to try to cheer fans up. IF THEY WIN THAT GAME, THEY'LL PLAY TESCO NEXT AND THEN ASDA AFTER THAT

What's the difference between England and a tea bag? THE TEA BAG STAYS IN THE CUP LONGER

My computer's got the Bad Goalie virus. IT CAN'T SAVE ANYTHING

Why did Cinderella get dropped from the football team? SHE KEPT RUNNING AWAY FROM THE BALL

BUILD THE...
PERFECT PLAYER!

Take the best bits of your favourite stars to create the ultimate player!

STRENGTH
Adebayo Akinfenwa

Zlatan Ibrahimovic

Wes Morgan

Christopher Samba

Victor Wanyama

Other: fill in below...

HEADING
Aritz Aduriz

Andy Carroll

Cristiano Ronaldo

Sergio Ramos

Alvaro Morata

Other: fill in below...

PASSING
Kevin De Bruyne

Christian Eriksen

Cesc Fabregas

Toni Kroos

Mesut Ozil

Other: fill in below...

SPEED

P-E Aubameyang

Gareth Bale

Hector Bellerin

Leroy Sane

Jamie Vardy

Other: fill in below...

SHOOTING

Harry Kane

Robert Lewandowski

Lionel Messi

Cristiano Ronaldo

Luis Suarez

Other: fill in below...

DRIBBLING

Paulo Dybala

Eden Hazard

Lionel Messi

Neymar

Cristiano Ronaldo

Other: fill in below...

DEFENDING

Andrea Barzagli

Giorgio Chiellini

Mats Hummels

Sergio Ramos

Thiago Silva

Other: fill in below...

HAVE YOU PICKED YOUR STAR FOR EACH CATEGORY? NOW TURN OVER TO CREATE YOUR ULTIMATE PLAYER!

MY PERFECT PLAYER!

Now put your perfect player together. They'd be world beaters!

HEADING

STRENGTH

PASSING

SPEED

SHOOTING

DRIBBLING

DEFENDING

EXTRA-TIME!

ET

You thought it was all over, but it's not quite. Here's a few extra quizzes!

WORDSEARCH

Try to find these 20 recent Serie A stars in the grid!

Barzagli	Benatia
Bonucci	Chiellini
Dybala	Hamsik
Handanovic	Higuain
Insigne	Khedira

Koulibaly	Marchisio
Matuidi	Mertens
Miranda	Nainggolan
Perisic	Pjanic
Sandro	Strootman

J X D H C H Q B A I R G D U E K P J K
H I O U X G Z S T R O O T M A N L T J
P X P T N H A J Y V M T P K L O Q E H
R A Z Z E J Z A W G S A T C Z H Z L U
M A T U I D I X U D I P I R S Z Y R P
X X P V R H A D V Z H E B N D N I L A
C Q Y F K X P J A N I C C S S W V P C
G T K P W M H I G U A I N Y I I N C M
N I H A N D A N O V I C O W R E G M X
A L E A P J Z B S E U Y Z Q U C G N H
I K D Q N X V B L V O E
N R I B N L N W M K B X
G U R C E E  A F F Z O U
G N A K V A K F Q A N I
O E V I L N S R Q V U G
L E G A R V J A I E C J
A I B G I A N J F O C K
N Y J J K D Z C S V I V
D O M F B X A Q C H I E L L I N I S R
S X I V K P E R I S I C C N R X H D W
B E N A T I A X Q B A P R I C W L L S
Z H H Y M A R C H I S I O B H D G R F
Z L R D K V K O U L I B A L Y A D P M
J P E Y T K V B A R Z A G L I S G O I
W E J H H L X O K I H Y X B L Z N A R
Q L M E R T E N S U H H A M S I K P A
P R R F O E X I Y B J E M S O G K N N
V X E D F E S A N D R O W E E J N Y D
T B Y F V I G O X U T H B U W P R A A

TRUE or FALSE?

Which of these statements are true, and which ones are totally made up?

1 The first ever World Cup was played way back in 1930.

2 South American giants Uruguay won the first two World Cup competitions.

3 The World Cup finals have never been held in France.

4 In 1966, the World Cup was stolen and then found by a dog called Pickles.

5 The wicked World Cup finals are held every five years.

WHO AM I?

Use the clues to work out this World Cup winner.

↘ I play for one of Spain's biggest clubs.

↘ I'm a midfield pass master.

↘ I scored the winner in the 2010 final.

SOCCER SCRAMBLE

Rearrange the letters to reveal a goalscoring superstar!

A N _ _ I E _ E

G R _ Z _ N N

What Nationality?

Which countries do these goal machines come from? We've done one to start you off!

1

Mohamed Salah

2

Ousmane Dembele

3

Edinson Cavani

4

Gonzalo Higuain

A

France

B

Uruguay

C

Argentina

D

Egypt

1. nd D

MATCH! 169

IN THE BOX!

How much do you know about the France national side?

1. In which year did France last lift the World Cup trophy?

A	2006	
B	1998	✓
C	1990	

4. What is the nickname of the France international football team?

A	The Blues	✓
B	The Chickens	
C	The Team	

2. Which awesome player is France's all-time record goalscorer?

A	Karim Benzema	
B	Michel Platini	
C	Thierry Henry	✓

3. How many times have France won the European Championships?

A	1
B	2
C	3

What is France's young Barcelona striker called?

A	Mousa Dembele	
B	Moussa Dembele	
C	Ousmane Dembele	✓

PETER CROUCH

MAMADOU SAKHO

PHILIPPE COUTINHO

CLUB SHARERS!

★ ★ ★ ★ ★ ★ ★ ★

Which top Premier League club have these stars all played for?

Liverpool

LUIS SUAREZ

RAHEEM STERLING

JOE ALLEN

PREMIER LEAGUE...

ANAGRAMS!

Rearrange the letters to find the Prem heroes!

1. LAMEUN LINZINA

2. DAIRY HEARZM

3. SUCRAM SADHORRF

4. GRILBAE USSEJ

5. CHRISTINA NEKSIRE

WHO AM I?

Which Premier League superstar is this?

↘ I started my career at Sporting Lisbon.   ↘ I joined Tottenham in 2014 for £4 million.   ↘ I scored for England at Euro 2016.

FINAL WHISTLE!

FT

That's all, folks! Turn over to check your answers and see how well you did!

QUIZ ANSWERS!

Now it's time to check out how many quizzes you got right!

PREMIER LEAGUE... Wordsearch

```
R  V  X  U  X  W  E  S  T  H  A  M  D  T  W  A  V  D  Z
D  L  B  J  B  E  K  E  E  K  N  G  Z  Z  S  F  N  R  V
K  E  U  C  N  L  E  I  C  E  S  T  E  R  J  W  E  G  V
J  E  R  Y  O  I  Q  E  W  E  E  C  Q  B  T  X  W  Z  J
J  D  N  X  T  A  Z  C  E  D  J  D  M  G  T  J  C  B  E
E  S  L  Z  T  A  X  B  S  K  O  I  P  B  A  V  A  T  X
M  B  E  D  I  F  D  Y  T  B  Y  F  X  G  R  D  S  M  W
A  V  Y  X  N  U  C  J  B  Z  G  K  K  H  S  U  T  A  H
N  O  X  L  G  L  H  Z  R  P  W  Q  J  W  E  O  L  N  P
C  Y  N  X  H  H  E  L  O  C  S  H  H  Z  N  C  E  C  K
H  C  M  K  A  A  L  O  M  U  X  O  K  J  A  Z  U  H  P
E  T  L  D  M  M  S  W  S  K  Z  L  I  L  L  R  L  E  S
S  O  I  M  F  B  E  W  I  J  G  Q  R  L  F  A  I  S  N
T  T  V  D  O  D  A  V  C  K  N  K  P  O  C  Q  X  T  I
E  T  E  S  R  Z  Z  O  H  A  T  N  G  O  X  Q  R  E  N
R  E  R  F  E  N  Q  T  A  R  S  H  Q  V  X  Q  Q  R  I
U  N  P  N  S  C  Y  Y  L  R  M  T  S  C  G  M  Q  C  K
N  H  O  H  T  N  G  A  B  I  I  F  O  M  Z  H  B  I  W
I  A  J  K  F  I  Y  I  O  D  H  U  N  E  X  Z  T  D
T  M  L  P  W  M  E  F  O  J  D  U  T  B  V  I  Q  Y  A
E  X  L  R  Y  O  W  E  N  S  L  R  H  H  Q  I  W  V  E
D  K  W  M  H  S  Q  A  Q  X  E  G  A  S  E  P  L  C  U
Y  I  J  J  N  N  E  K  U  P  S  U  M  W  V  H  S  L  E
N  V  Y  D  A  S  F  B  P  B  B  Y  P  A  E  A  A  M  A
M  Q  A  U  N  W  G  N  R  U  R  J  T  T  R  I  M  H
W  R  P  A  U  N  B  K  A  O  O  Q  O  F  T  A  Q  U  Y
D  I  W  E  Q  L  C  K  A  D  U  O  N  O  E  T  W  C
K  S  P  G  W  H  Q  X  D  U  G  Q  W  R  N  E  H  K  L
X  P  S  H  W  D  W  P  B  T  H  I  X  D  W  W  D  J  R
```

14-15	16-17

WORLD CUP... Club Sharers:
Barcelona

**WORLD CUP...
Nickname Game:**
1. C
2. A
3. E
4. B
5. D

GOAL KINGS... Fill The Spaces:
1. Morata – Spain
2. Kane – England
3. Mbappe – France
4. Lukaku – Belgium
5. Aguero – Argentina
6. Aubameyang – Gabon

GOAL KINGS... Who Am I?
Luis Suarez

22-23

FA CUP...
Odd One Out:
Sergio Aguero

FA CUP...
True or False?
1. False
2. True
3. False
4. False
5. True

18-19

BARCELONA...
Lionel Messi Quiz:
1. 1987
2. 2004
3. 2006
4. 10
5. True

20-21

SERIE A...
Name The Country:
1. Dybala – Argentina
2. Hamsik – Slovakia
3. Nainggolan – Belgium
4. Miranda – Brazil
5. Nani – Portugal
6. Reina – Spain
7. Manolas – Greece
8. Khedira – Germany

SERIE A... Transfer Tracker:
2016-present – Juventus

24-25

WORLD STARS...
Gareth Bale Quiz:
1. 1989
2. Southampton
3. One
4. Martin Jol
5. True

26-27

MAN. UNITED...
True or False?
1. True
2. True
3. False
4. False
5. False

MAN. UNITED...
Guess The Year:
1. 2013
2. 2016
3. 2008
4. 2013

28-29

LA LIGA... Flip For It:
1. Real Madrid
2. Filipe Luis
3. Athletic Bilbao
4. Espanyol
5. Valencia
6. Lionel Messi

LA LIGA...
Name The Club:
Atletico Madrid

30-31

CHAMPIONS LEAGUE...
Grounded:
1. PSG
2. Atletico Madrid
3. Man. City
4. Juventus

32-33

LEGENDS... Who Am I?
Dennis Bergkamp

LEGENDS...
Who Started Where?
1. C
2. D
3. A
4. B

34-35

BUNDESLIGA...
Nickname Game:
1. B
2. D
3. E
4. A
5. C

BUNDESLIGA...
Soccer Scramble:
Eintracht Frankfurt

180

REAL MADRID... Wordsearch

```
P E C J A T J N N G U U L Z T H V V X
C T Z S Z D U B A L E Y I Q I J N P Q
Y P V W B R B R V I E U M M Z R P G S
P U I X Z G K U F L T U P L M M C A H
D D L C S B O C T R H N W E R W K M M
P U J L P E W L O R V Q O K B S Z Z X
U Q U M E N I I N V A Y J B U E I I M
Q J S S J Z W H V G C G R P D I V A A
T R Y X M E T R O Y Q A U A C H N E R
K F M L A M H K U H V B M E U Z I N C
Z R C T W A F N L M E O N E L
I P Y J K P K N O U N L O
H L C X X G J G L R I O S
K L O J K E C M F L Q S
R K U J Z E R N H H V J
U U U K O Y S C K Q R H
Y B P Z T Y A A Q T A M B
C M A Y Y A L S Z Z M B
A O E Y R O G I V O O S
R D L G P Q F I S W G O R A L H Q S K
L R H W F H E L G U E R A D L P C Q E
O I I F D I S T E F A N O O A I C Z D
S C D P J J G T S O T Q L Y S L H X H
V G E T E C D O H I E R R O A S H Z J
I D J J A E A X J X S V E Z Q S I C O
Q Q Q H Y Z M O J O H I G U A I N P X
Z N H G K Z A M O R A N O C G T V E Y
L I I Z C B T L M R P Q Z U A Y Z P B
C P M C C E U B I R O N A L D O J E L
```

38-39

INTERNATIONAL...
Club Sharers:
Chelsea

INTERNATIONAL...
What Nationality?
1. D
2. B
3. A
4. C

40-41

WONDERKIDS...
Name The Country:
1. Woodburn – Wales
2. Pulisic – USA
3. Hernandez – France
4. Dolberg – Denmark
5. Sancho – England
6. Ndidi – Nigeria
7. Donnarumma – Italy
8. Meyer – Germany

WONDERKIDS...
Who Am I?
Marcus Rashford

42-43

MAN. CITY...
First XI:
1. Etihad Stadium
2. Pep Guardiola
3. 2011-12
4. Sergio Aguero
5. Citizens
6. Maine Road
7. Stoke
8. Roberto Mancini
9. Brazil
10. Liverpool
11. Nike

44-45

FOOTBALL LEAGUE...
Fill The Spaces:
1. Derby County
2. Portsmouth
3. Leeds United
4. Plymouth Argyle
5. Accrington Stanley

FOOTBALL LEAGUE...
Name The Club:
Hull City

46-47

WORLD CUP... Odd One Out:
Shkodran Mustafi

WORLD CUP...
Flip For It:
1. Once
2. Qatar
3. 1998
4. Spain
5. Germany
6. Japan & South Korea

48-49

GOAL KINGS... Wordfit

```
      H
      I
      G I R O U D               L
G     U                         U
R O N A L D O                   K
I     I             C O S T A   A
E     N E Y M A R             K
Z   D               J E S U S
M   Y     L     C     A   U
A U B A M E Y A N G     K A N E
N   A     W     V     U   R
N   L   L A C A Z E T T E   Z
    A     N     N     R   Z
          D     I     R
          O           O
      M   W
      O   W
      O R A S H F O R D
      A   K                 M
      T   I M M O B I L E S
      A                     S
                            S
                            I
```

50-51

PSG... Who Am I?
Kylian Mbappe

PSG... What Nationality?
1. D
2. C
3. A
4. B

52-53

PREMIER LEAGUE...
Name The Club:
Man. United

PREMIER LEAGUE...
Nickname Game:
1. E
2. A
3. C
4. B
5. D

54-55

FA CUP... Action Replay:
1. Alexis Sanchez
2. David Ospina
3. 1-0 to Arsenal
4. Victor Moses
5. 2-1 to Arsenal

56-57

WORLD STARS...
Soccer Scramble:
Arjen Robben

WORLD STARS...
Who Started Where?
1. D
2. B
3. A
4. C

58-59

CHELSEA... True or False?
1. True
2. False
3. True
4. True
5. False

CHELSEA... What Nationality?
1. C
2. A
3. D
4. B

LA LIGA... Wordsearch

```
H V R T Q H E W Z I S S E M A B N Z A
R P Q Y C N D E I B R U N O D Z Q P I
S P Y N P B Q O B W U D N L U Y G D A
A I H Q Y I M F T J P N V Y R X P T O
V K T X E P S E K B A D C Z I I G S K
A P N V Z S B K O M Y V N Q Z O Z A N
N U T C R N C A Z N W B A B L L Y P A
I C C A P D W E G A U V F G K H E S I
Y T S R O D I U J U T Y J V O H Z A D
D L E R Q R Z D E V U F F S K R J Z N
B J Z A G F V E S M M E
B W R A S F F T Z R Z R A
Y I A C L W U Z X I A A
G U M O C D L S J V K R
S Q O D J F E C A A I R
B D S K Y S Z F L H T A
F Q E P U G H B M T I L
E A P Z O E O B G S C L
Q Q Y J Y G C H C U L I
V O A N G C D R I T U N X P F G A N C
L D X I V P J J Z N U T G F Y P R T E
Z L G Y T L T G Q N U M Q V P Z E A V
T A H U I U B K R O O S V R V A Z F O
P N R K W I L L I A M S P I K Z K W J
H O E B J L I B O P Y A O E R A L J E
X R H V L Q T K Q A I A R Z G B S B R
B W U A A D N Y Q X X L K Z D I E K A
X K T V Q M S P D O N A I R O S K H P
N O Z R K Z N W C M Y G J Y K G E U P
```

66-67

JUVENTUS... QUIZ:
1. The Old Lady
2. Notts County
3. Turin
4. 1897
5. Paul Pogba
(to Man. United for £90 million)

68-69

SERIE A...
Nickname Game:
1. E
2. A
3. B
4. C
5. D

SERIE A...
Name The Club:
Roma

62-63

CHAMPIONS LEAGUE...
Club Sharers:
Lyon

CHAMPIONS LEAGUE...
True or False?
1. True
2. False
3. True
4. False
5. True

70-71

INTERNATIONAL...
True or False?
1. True
2. True
3. True
4. False
5. False

INTERNATIONAL...
Soccer Scramble:
Ivory Coast

64-65

LEGENDS... Fill The Spaces:
1. David Beckham
2. Ronaldo
3. Didier Drogba
4. Thierry Henry
5. Francesco Totti

72-73

WONDERKIDS... Wordfit

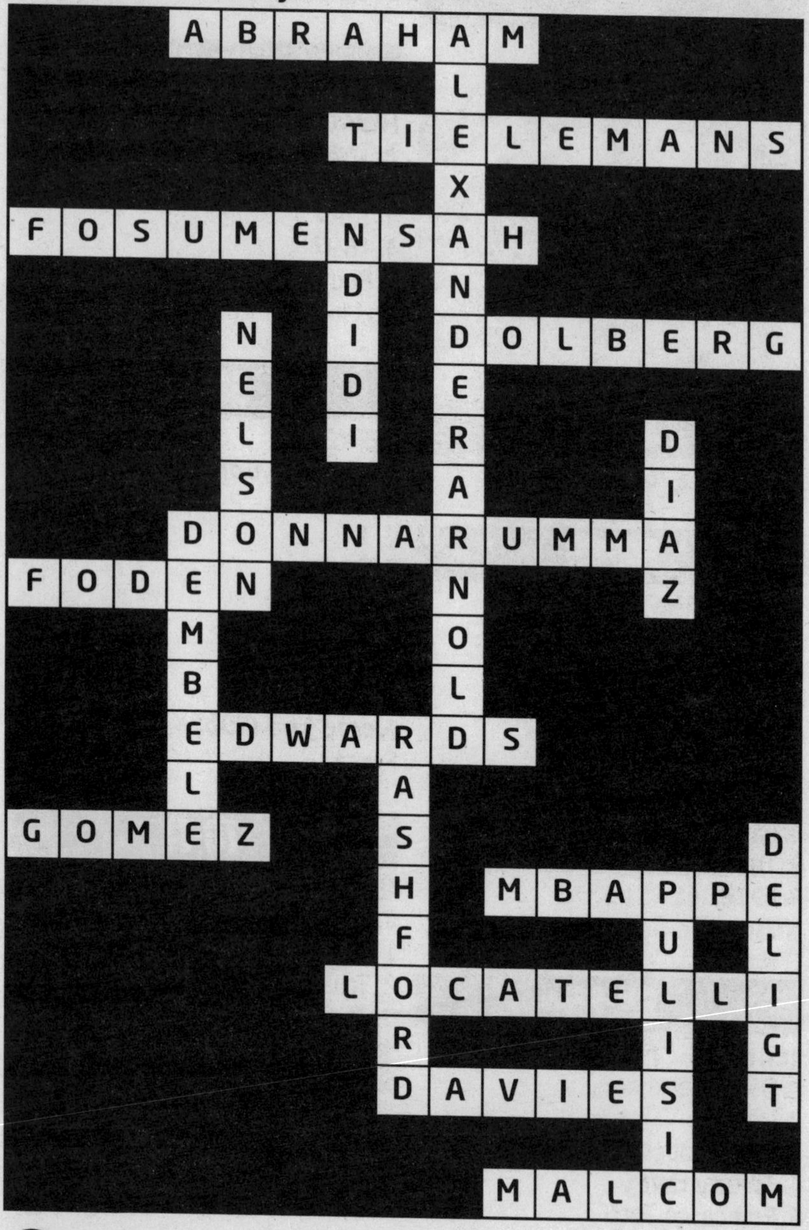

ABRAHAM

TIELEMANS

FOSUMENSAH

DOLBERG

NELSON

DONNARUMMA

DIAZ

FODEN

EDWARDS

GOMEZ

MBAPPE

LOCATELLI

DAVIES

MALCOM

74-75

ARSENAL... Who Am I?
Alexandre Lacazette

ARSENAL... Flip For It:
1. Thierry Henry
2. Highbury
3. £16 million
4. Swiss
5. 13
6. Schalke

76-77

FOOTBALL LEAGUE...
Nickname Game:
1. B
2. D
3. E
4. A
5. C

FOOTBALL LEAGUE...
Odd One Out:
Britt Assombalonga

FOOTBALL LEAGUE...
Club Sharers:
Sunderland

88-89

WORLD CUP...
Action Replay:
1. 7-1 to Germany
2. Black and red hoops
3. Semi-final
4. True
5. Five

90-91

GOAL KINGS...
True or False?
1. True
2. True
3. False
4. True
5. False

GOAL KINGS...
Who Started Where?
1. B
2. C
3. A
4. D

92-93

BAYERN MUNICH...
Anagrams:
1. Manuel Neuer
2. Arturo Vidal
3. Mats Hummels
4. Thomas Muller
5. David Alaba

BAYERN MUNICH...
Who Am I?
Robert Lewandowski

94-95

PREMIER LEAGUE...
In The Box:
1. B
2. A
3. B
4. C
5. A

96-97

FA CUP... Soccer Scramble:
Wigan Athletic

FA CUP... Odd One Out:
Jamie Vardy

98-99

WORLD STARS...
Club Sharers:
Juventus

WORLD STARS...
Who Am I?
Philippe Coutinho

LIVERPOOL... Wordsearch

```
G O F W G K L G W J P D T J I F O V H
F O W L E R X F R J H X D F C I Y S H
R V M M X S R E I N A W B Q D J C A E
K S F J N A H A M A N N L H D V N L E
M A U O X K U H V M L J U Y S C B D R
B Y V K H A S C D A L G L I S H Z R U
L I I P K Y O Y G T L M Y T V W J I S
D V Y M N B E A R D S L E Y T H A D H
U W W B W L G A N M R Y R Z M O C G V
D K N G Y N R K P P O Q H U L A V E V
E Y P P G E Y U C S R R
K D C L D R S Y W O C N
P X S R H A V J P V O D
E A X L Y Z B R P I Q P
C W K A X C B A Q B Z A K
N W Q J R O V C N N U P
G N W K U U C P J H B I
O E R D E T N T P G C W
D C F X B I S D Z H V R
N C Z M W N N V P W I D P F V U D V E
F F N X Q H Y M O M C J D G N Z S P Z
A L O N S O J Z D W M X I E E V B Y G
F S G T O R R E S B E R Q R N T A Z U
C S V E G D G K T Q O N A R I R R M W
G K U R Z F B P Z V I U L A B A N O E
W C A R R A G H E R S J D R Z T E B Y
C Z V H E N D E R S O N Q D R W S Y Y
W Q H D U J T M T K E K K S U P R P W
H S A L A H W C W M A S C H E R A N O
```

102-103

BUNDESLIGA... Fill The Spaces:
1. Borussia Dortmund
2. Hoffenheim
3. Bayern Munich
4. Wolfsburg
5. Bayer Leverkusen

**BUNDESLIGA...
Transfer Tracker:**
2015-present – Bayern Munich

104-105

LEGENDS... Name The Country:
1. Zidane – France
2. Raul – Spain
3. Batistuta – Argentina
4. Figo – Portugal
5. Forlan – Uruguay
6. Ronaldo – Brazil
7. Valderrama – Colombia
8. Maradona – Argentina

LEGENDS... Who Am I?
Alan Shearer

106-107

CHAMPIONS LEAGUE... Quiz:
1. Chelsea
2. Real Madrid
3. Juventus
4. AC Milan
5. True

108-109

**ATLETICO MADRID...
Odd One Out:**
Stefan Savic

ATLETICO MADRID... Who Am I?
Diego Godin

110-111

LA LIGA... Nickname Game:
1. D
2. E
3. A
4. B
5. C

LA LIGA... What Nationality?
1. B
2. C
3. D
4. A

112-113

INTERNATIONAL... Wordfit

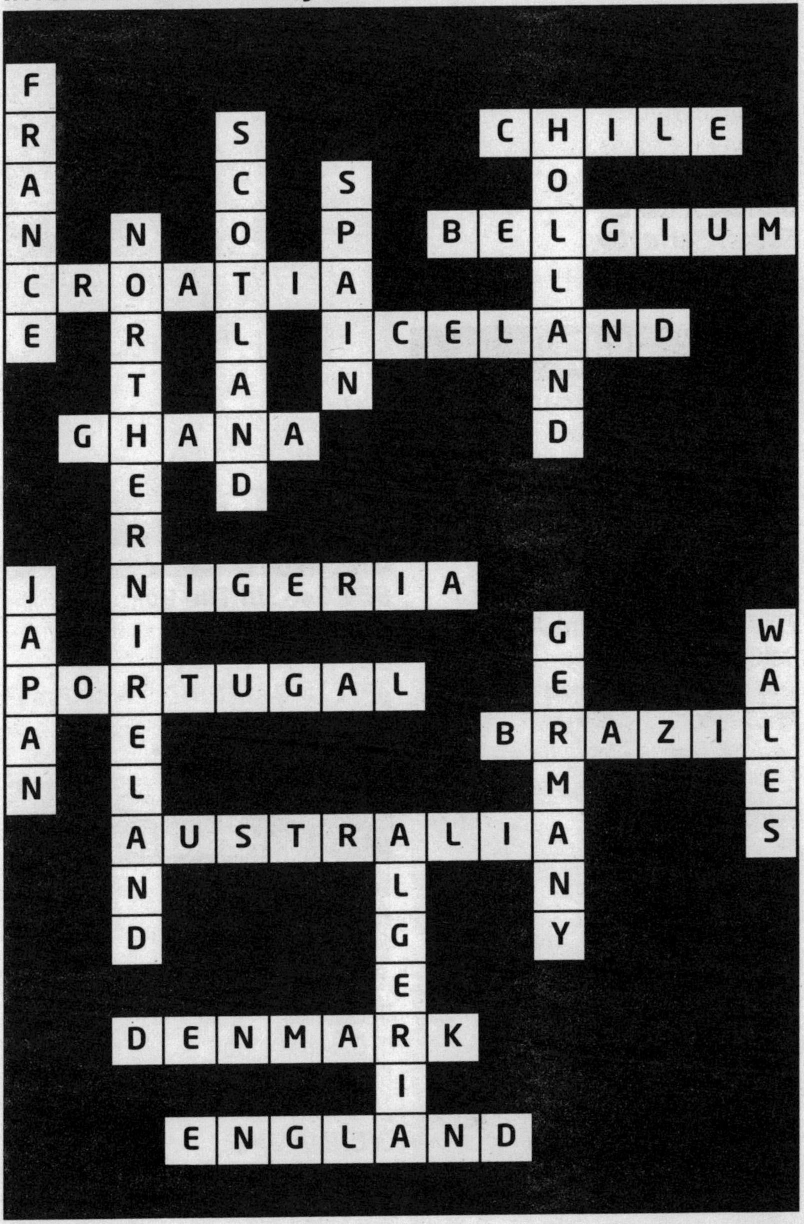

FRANCE
SCOTLAND
CHILE
SPAIN
BELGIUM
HOLLAND
NORTHERN IRELAND
CROATIA
ICELAND
GHANA
JAPAN
NIGERIA
GERMANY
WALES
PORTUGAL
BRAZIL
AUSTRALIA
ALGERIA
DENMARK
ENGLAND

114-115

WONDERKIDS...
What Nationality?
1. D
2. B
3. A
4. C

WONDERKIDS...
Soccer Scramble:
Phil Foden

116-117

TOTTENHAM... Anagrams:
1. Harry Kane
2. Victor Wanyama
3. Hugo Lloris
4. Toby Alderweireld
5. Danny Rose

TOTTENHAM... Who Am I?
Dele Alli

118-119

SERIE A... In The Box:
1. C
2. A
3. C
4. B
5. C

120-121

WORLD CUP...
Fill The Spaces:
1. Eden Hazard
2. Toni Kroos
3. Neymar
4. Gerard Pique
5. Hugo Lloris

WORLD CUP...
Transfer Tracker:
2013-present – Arsenal

122-123

GOAL KINGS... Odd One Out:
Zlatan Ibrahimovic

GOAL KINGS...True or False?
1. False
2. True
3. False
4. True
5. False

124-125

ENGLAND...
Action Replay:
1. Raheem Sterling
2. Wayne Rooney
3. 2-1 to Iceland
4. False
5. Joe Hart

126-127

FOOTBALL LEAGUE...
True or False?
1. True
2. False
3. False
4. True
5. False

FOOTBALL LEAGUE...
Guess The Year:
Newcastle - 2016-17
Burnley - 2015-16
Bournemouth - 2014-15
Leicester - 2013-14

128-129

FA CUP... Fill The Spaces:
1. Arsenal
2. Manchester United
3. Wigan Athletic
4. Chelsea
5. Manchester City

FA CUP... Who Am I?
Petr Cech

WORLD STARS... Wordsearch

```
Q P D S I K Z P Q I E F H G L Y J B P
X W M H I U U Z B Q O C P I X V H A L
W Y P G T E M Q R G G X J I K D V O T
H V Q O D H S V A Z V S C A V A N I A
N S V N Z S R X Z G R I E Z M A N N H
W J R T V X E L M R Z H F G S T I P D
K V C R E L J P O G B A V H S M M F R
X A S Z A Y N D K A N T E D U Q C W K
Q G N B Q R N M L E W A N D O W S K I
Y E A E X R P R D H U R Z M Z M Y N R
C F R O N A L D O F S A L A H V R M E
Z B L V C G                I K O P Q M
Z X L O R F                I W Y B U B
B A Q E K L                D Q O R Q A
R P O Z D G                C D K B B P
Z J R F G G                S M D J A P
B K P A O M                X K C Z T E
R Z V M S Z                T R O R Y C
M V F A L S U K S Q L D E B R U Y N E
O O T E M X Q P R N Z K L R A M O S I
D E E Q W Q G M Z O V E J W Z D H G N
R S Z U L C P X U W O N T O H Y W M Q
I S C O I R O L J J V S S A A B P R C
C R Z F D J D U W A D W B M Z A X A K
O N E Y M A R X T C N D E E A L A W U
F H B M E S S I Q I U L H B R A V C U
U Z B R V L R O W J N M I U D Z Y Y C
H T T M V U H G K W Q H S F K Q Q G W
C C M F U M Y F R J A C O I H C Q A B
```

132-133

BRAZIL... Odd One Out:
Fernandinho

BRAZIL... True or False?
1. True
2. False
3. False
4. True
5. True

134-135

PREMIER LEAGUE... Who Am I?
Kyle Walker

**PREMIER LEAGUE...
Who Started Where?**
1. A
2. C
3. D
4. B

136-137

CHAMPIONS LEAGUE... First XI:
1. 32
2. Liverpool
3. Barcelona
4. Liverpool
5. Man. United & Chelsea
6. Man. United
7. Two
8. False
9. 2013
10. Real Madrid
11. Cristiano Ronaldo

138-139

**GOAL KINGS...
What Nationality?**
1. B
2. D
3. C
4. A

**GOAL KINGS...
Transfer Tracker:**
2013-17 – Everton

140-141

SPAIN... Anagrams:
1. David De Gea
2. Alvaro Morata
3. Sergio Ramos
4. Diego Costa
5. Jordi Alba

SPAIN...
Flip For It:
1. Sergio Ramos
2. Andres Iniesta
3. 4-0
4. Julen Lopetegui
5. David Silva
6. Atletico Madrid

142-143

BUNDESLIGA... Wordfit

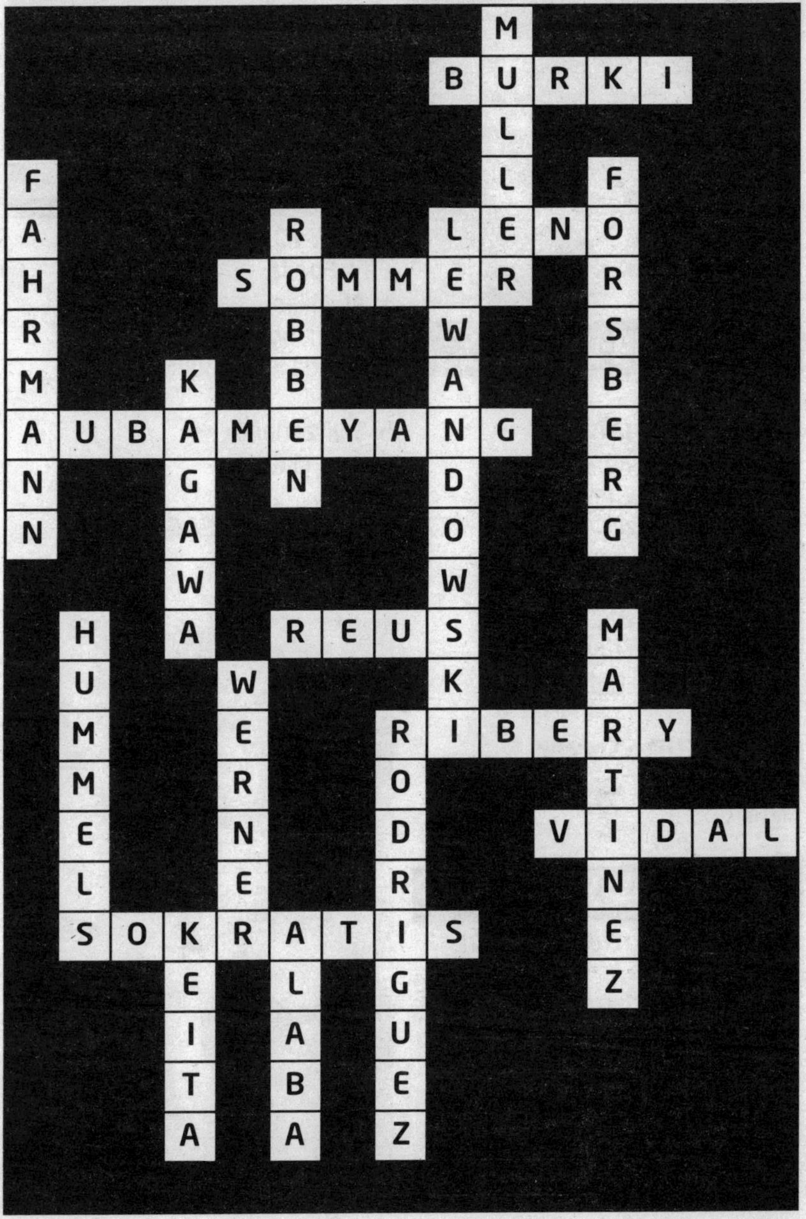
MULLER
BURKI
LENO
FORSBERG
ROBBEN
SOMMER
LEWANDOWSKI
FAHRMANN
KAGAWA
AUBAMEYANG
REUS
HUMMELS
WERNER
MARTINEZ
RIBERY
RODRIGUEZ
VIDAL
SOKRATIS
KEITA
ALABA

144-145

WORLD CUP...
Name The Country:
1. Okazaki – Japan
2. Suarez – Uruguay
3. Nani – Portugal
4. Busquets – Spain
5. Fernandinho – Brazil
6. Rakitic – Croatia
7. Hernandez – Mexico
8. Nainggolan – Belgium

WORLD CUP... Soccer
Scramble:
Mario Gotze

146-147

ARGENTINA... Odd One Out:
Angel Di Maria

ARGENTINA... True or False?
1. False
2. True
3. False
4. True
5. False

148-149

LA LIGA... Grounded:
1. Barcelona
2. Valencia
3. Villarreal
4. Real Madrid

150-151

CHAMPIONS LEAGUE...
Flip For It:
1. AC Milan
2. Cristiano Ronaldo
3. Wanda Metropolitano
4. No
5. Switzerland
6. Real Madrid

CHAMPIONS LEAGUE...
Who Am I?
Sergio Ramos

152-153

LEGENDS...
Name The Country:
1. Giggs - Wales
2. Deco - Portugal
3. Salgado - Spain
4. Totti - Italy
5. Bergkamp - Holland
6. Ballack - Germany
7. Romario - Brazil
8. Keane - Rep. Of Ireland

LEGENDS...
Soccer Scramble:
Gary Lineker

154

LEGENDS...
What Nationality?
1. B
2. A
3. D
4. C

SERIE A... Wordsearch

```
J X D H C H Q B A I R G D U E K P J K
H I O U X G Z S T R O O T M A N L T J
P X P T N H A J Y V M T P K L O Q E H
R A Z Z E J Z A W G S A T C Z H Z L U
M A T U I D I X U D I P I R S Z Y R P
X X P V R H A D V Z H E B N D N I L A
C Q Y F K X P J A N I C C S S W V P C
G T K P W M H I G U A I N Y I I N C M
N I H A N D A N O V I C O W R E G M X
A L E A P J Z B S E U Y Z Q U C G N H
I K D Q N X V B L V O E
N R I B N L N W M K B K
G U R C E E A F F Z O U
G N A K V A K F Q A N I
O E V I L N S R Q V U G
L E G A R V J A I E C J
A I B G I A N J F O C K
N Y J J K D Z C S V I V
D O M F B X A Q C H I E L L I N I S R
S X I V K P E R I S I C C N R X H D W
B E N A T I A X Q B A P R I C W L L S
Z H H Y M A R C H I S I O B H D G R F
Z L R D K V K O U L I B A L Y A D P M
J P E Y T K V B A R Z A G L I S G O I
W E J H L X O K I H Y X B L Z N A R
Q L M E R T E N S U H H A M S I K P A
P R R F O E X I Y B J E M S O G K N N
V X E D F E S A N D R O W E E J N Y D
T B Y F V I G O X U T H B U W P R A A
```

166-167

WORLD CUP... True or False?
1. True
2. False
3. False
4. True
5. False

WORLD CUP... Who Am I?
Andres Iniesta

168-169

GOAL KINGS...
Soccer Scramble:
Antoine Griezmann

GOAL KINGS...
What Nationality?
1. D
2. A
3. B
4. C

170-171

FRANCE... In The Box:
1. B
2. C
3. B
4. A
5. C

172-173

PREMIER LEAGUE...
Club Sharers:
Liverpool

PREMIER LEAGUE... Anagrams:
1. Manuel Lanzini
2. Riyad Mahrez
3. Marcus Rashford
4. Gabriel Jesus
5. Christian Eriksen

174

PREMIER LEAGUE... Who Am I?
Eric Dier

MATCH! INCREDIBLE STATS & FACTS

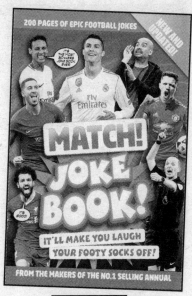

MATCH! JOKE BOOK

MATCH! WORLD CUP DIARY 2018

MATCH! BUILD YOUR OWN CLUB

TO ORDER, GO TO: WWW.PANMACMILLAN.COM